INSIDE GUIDES

FOREST

Written by
DAVID BURNIE

FAMILY LEARNING

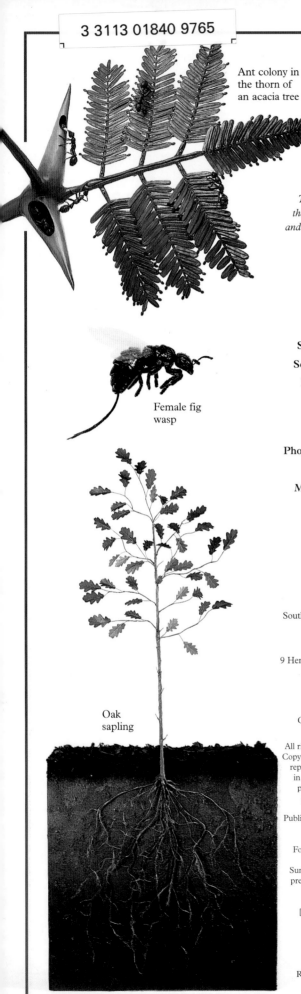

Ant colony in the thorn of an acacia tree

Female fig wasp

Oak sapling

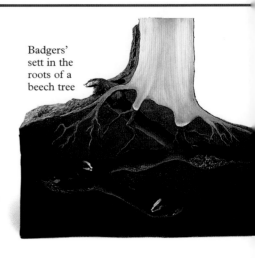

Badgers' sett in the roots of a beech tree

FL
FAMILY LEARNING

from Dorling Kindersely

The Family Learning mission is to support the concept of the home as a center of learning and to help families develop independent learning skills to last a lifetime.

Editor Carey Scott
US editor William Lach
Designer Janet Allis
DTP designer Nicola Studdart
Senior managing editor Linda Martin
Senior managing art editor Julia Harris
Picture research Catherine Costelloe
Production Lisa Moss
Jacket design Dean Price

Photography Geoff Brightling, Steve Gorton, and Andy Crawford
Modelmakers Peter Minister Model FX, Chris Reynolds and the BBC team, and Gary and Lissi Staab

First American edition, 1998
2 4 6 8 10 9 7 5 3 1

Published by Family Learning

Southland Executive Park, 7800 Southland Boulevard, Orlando, Florida 32809.

Dorling Kindersley registered offices:
9 Henrietta Street, Covent Garden, London WC2E 8PS

VISIT US ON THE WORLD WIDE WEB AT:
http://www.dk.com

Published in Great Britain by Dorling Kindersley Limited.

Burnie, David
Forest / written by David Burnie. -- 1st American ed.
p. cm. -- (Inside guides)
Summary: Text, photographs, and cutaway illustrations present the forest, its inhabitants, and their interaction.
ISBN 0-7894-3492-X (alk. paper)
1. Forest ecology--Juvenile literature.
[1. Forest ecology. 2. Ecology.] I. Title II. Series.
QH541.5.F6B86 1998
577.3--dc21   98-17808
                    CIP
                    AC

Reproduced in Italy by GRB Editrice, S.r.l., Verona
Printed in Singapore by Toppan

Pine forest

Deadly honey fungus

Bud of a
chestnut tree

Contents

Female pine
cone

Creatures living in
the leaf litter

Forests of the world

Tough leaves
Small, leathery leaves can slough off snow, withstand cold, and retain moisture.

In some parts of the world, particularly where it is very dry, trees find it difficult to survive. But where there is enough light and moisture, they grow in huge numbers. The result is a forest – the richest and most complex natural habitat on dry land. At one time, forests covered more than a third of the Earth's land surface. Today, even after centuries of clearance for lumber and for farmland, they still dominate many parts of the globe. This book looks at the world of forests from the inside. It shows how forests vary, how their trees grow and reproduce, and how their plants and animals manage to thrive.

Cylindrical, glossy cones

Steady replacement
Dense, evergreen leaves are shed gradually throughout the year.

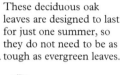

Short-lived leaves
These deciduous oak leaves are designed to last for just one summer, so they do not need to be as tough as evergreen leaves.

Coniferous forest
Conifers – trees that reproduce by making cones – are good at withstanding tough conditions, including low temperatures and strong winds. Their leaves are usually small and evergreen, and are so dense that they cast a deep shade. This means that few other plants can grow on the forest floor.

Catching the light
In summer, the leaves intercept most of the sunlight, so the forest floor is quite dim.

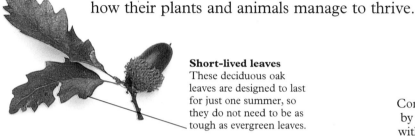

Canopy
The interlocking treetops form a layer called the canopy. In summer, it is full of insects and birds.

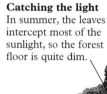

Forest floor
Shade-loving fungi often grow beneath conifers.

Deciduous forest
Trees in deciduous forests shed their leaves before winter begins and grow a new set in spring. The fallen leaves build up to form a layer called leaf litter. The deciduous forest floor is often covered in plants that flower before the trees come into leaf.

Drip tips
Tropical rainforest leaves often have sharp tips to help rainwater drain away.

High life
The tallest trees in rainforests can be over 230 ft (70 m) high.

Rainforest

Near the equator it is wet and warm enough for trees to grow year round. Here, the trees are more varied than anywhere else on Earth. These tropical rainforests are home to immense numbers of animals, particularly insects.

In the shade
Low-growing palms survive in the deep shade on the forest floor.

Slender support
For their size, many of the biggest rainforest trees have quite slender trunks.

Forest map

This map shows the natural distribution of different kinds of forests. In many parts of the world, humans have reduced this natural spread by cutting down trees for lumber and to create land for farming or grazing.

Temperate deciduous forest
In most temperate regions, parts of the original forest have been cut down to leave a patchwork of woods. Woodlands are important places for wildlife.

Coniferous forest
The great boreal forest, which grows across North America, Scandinavia, and Russia, is the largest forest in the world. Much of the forest is still wilderness.

Rainforest
Tropical rainforests grow near the equator, and temperate rainforests are found on rain-soaked coasts in North America, South America, and New Zealand.

Fighting for light

From the moment it starts life on the forest floor, a young tree has one vital task to carry out: it has to get its share of the light. Without light, its leaves cannot collect energy, and without energy, the tree will die. If a tree germinates in the open, getting light is not a problem, but in the depths of a forest, things are not so simple. Here, trees are packed together, and the fight for light is deadly and intense. Most saplings lose the battle, but a few have better luck. If a nearby tree falls down, the canopy suddenly opens up, giving a young tree the light it needs to survive.

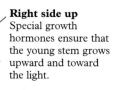

Right side up
Special growth hormones ensure that the young stem grows upward and toward the light.

Breaking up
The acorn's hard case splits open as the embryo germinates.

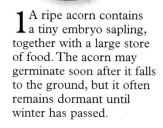

1 A ripe acorn contains a tiny embryo sapling, together with a large store of food. The acorn may germinate soon after it falls to the ground, but it often remains dormant until winter has passed.

Network of roots begins to develop

Shaded out
Mature beech trees have very dense foliage, so they cast unusually deep shade. In a mature beech wood, the forest floor can be almost empty, except in places where old trees have fallen down. Dead beech leaves create a deep layer of fertile leaf litter – an ideal compost for young saplings fortunate enough to germinate where there is light.

2 When it germinates, the young oak sapling relies on the food that is stored in the acorn. This food allows its stem to grow above the leaf litter – an essential first step in the struggle for light. Meanwhile, the tree's roots reach into the ground to absorb water and nutrients.

No-go zone
The gap between each crown is about 3 ft (1 m) wide.

Keep your distance
In tropical forests, the branches of neighboring trees are often separated by a narrow gap. This form of growth is called "crown shyness," because the trees seem to shy away from each other. Biologists do not know exactly why crown shyness occurs. One possibility is that it helps to stop leaf-eating caterpillars spreading from tree to tree.

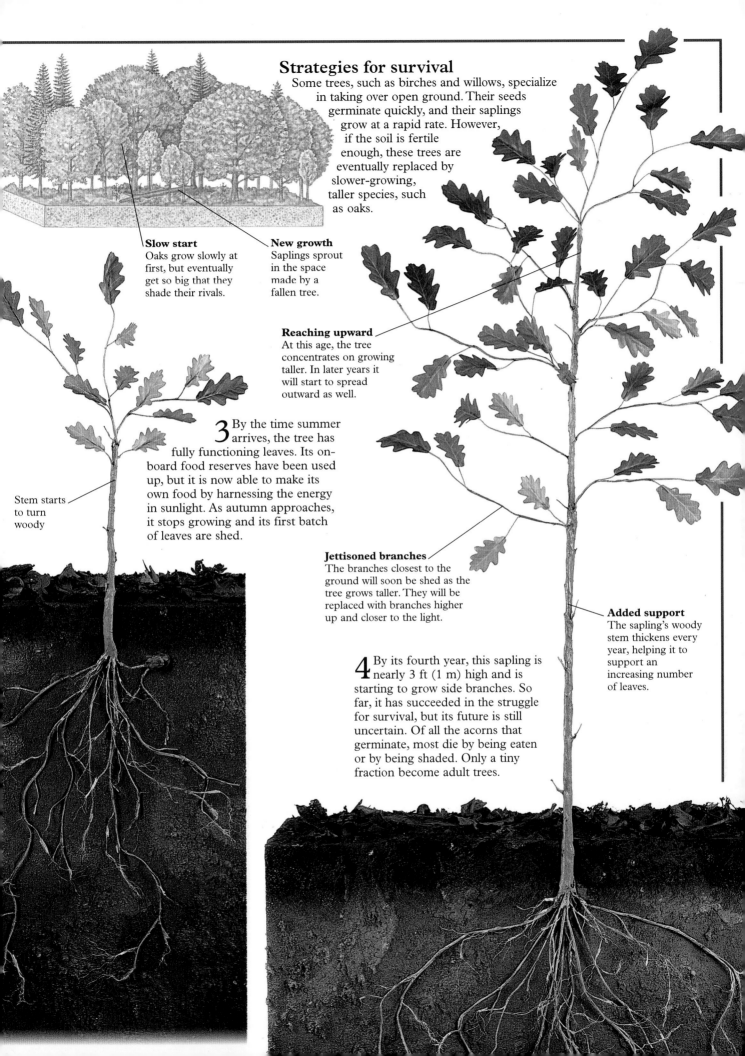

Strategies for survival

Some trees, such as birches and willows, specialize in taking over open ground. Their seeds germinate quickly, and their saplings grow at a rapid rate. However, if the soil is fertile enough, these trees are eventually replaced by slower-growing, taller species, such as oaks.

Slow start
Oaks grow slowly at first, but eventually get so big that they shade their rivals.

New growth
Saplings sprout in the space made by a fallen tree.

Reaching upward
At this age, the tree concentrates on growing taller. In later years it will start to spread outward as well.

3 By the time summer arrives, the tree has fully functioning leaves. Its on-board food reserves have been used up, but it is now able to make its own food by harnessing the energy in sunlight. As autumn approaches, it stops growing and its first batch of leaves are shed.

Stem starts to turn woody

Jettisoned branches
The branches closest to the ground will soon be shed as the tree grows taller. They will be replaced with branches higher up and closer to the light.

4 By its fourth year, this sapling is nearly 3 ft (1 m) high and is starting to grow side branches. So far, it has succeeded in the struggle for survival, but its future is still uncertain. Of all the acorns that germinate, most die by being eaten or by being shaded. Only a tiny fraction become adult trees.

Added support
The sapling's woody stem thickens every year, helping it to support an increasing number of leaves.

How leaves work

Leaves are like a tree's solar panels. They soak up the energy in sunlight and use it to make substances that the tree needs. These include the sugars, which make sap sticky and sweet, and also the materials that build wood, bark, and leaves themselves. To survive, trees need to absorb a lot of light, which means that they need lots of leaves. However, keeping all these leaves in working order is not an easy task. This is because leaves are often battered by the weather and may be attacked by hungry animals. Some of the most remarkable of these animals are tiny caterpillars called leaf miners. Chewing their way through leaves, they leave wiggling trails, or mines, that can be seen when an infected leaf is held up to the light.

Sugars travel from the leaves to all parts of the tree

Sunlight, containing useful energy, enters the leaf

Water travels up the tree trunk and enters the leaf

Carbon dioxide is absorbed from the air

The leaf gives off oxygen as a waste product

Fuel for trees

Leaves contain a green chemical called chlorophyll that captures the energy in sunlight. During a process called photosynthesis, leaves use this energy to turn water and carbon dioxide into a sugar called glucose, which is then used by the tree as a fuel.

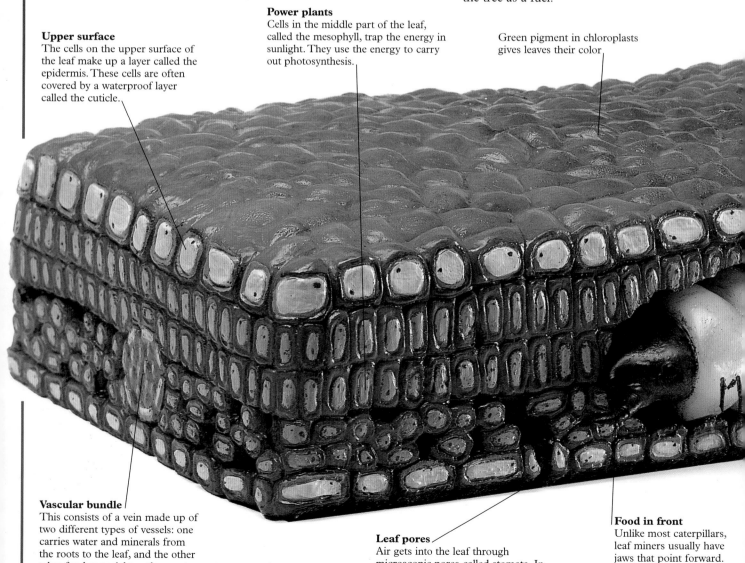

Power plants
Cells in the middle part of the leaf, called the mesophyll, trap the energy in sunlight. They use the energy to carry out photosynthesis.

Green pigment in chloroplasts gives leaves their color

Upper surface
The cells on the upper surface of the leaf make up a layer called the epidermis. These cells are often covered by a waterproof layer called the cuticle.

Vascular bundle
This consists of a vein made up of two different types of vessels: one carries water and minerals from the roots to the leaf, and the other takes food material to other parts of the tree.

Leaf pores
Air gets into the leaf through microscopic pores called stomata. In most trees, these pores open during the day and close at night.

Food in front
Unlike most caterpillars, leaf miners usually have jaws that point forward.

Types of leaves

Leaves all do the same work, but they vary enormously in shape and size. Some conifers have scalelike leaves just a sixteenth of an inch long, but palm leaves can be over 33 ft (10 m) from base to tip. Most leaves have a single flat blade, but in a compound leaf, the blade is divided up into lots of small units called leaflets.

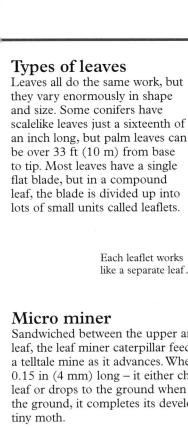

Kentucky coffee tree

Each leaflet works like a separate leaf

Magnolia

A tough, glossy surface is washed clean by rain

Fir

Tough, needle-like leaves are adapted to cope with very cold conditions. They even contain a built-in "antifreeze"

Maple

This flat, hand-shaped leaf is typical of maples

Willow

Narrow, lance-shaped leaf

Micro miner

Sandwiched between the upper and lower surfaces of a leaf, the leaf miner caterpillar feeds on leaf cells, leaving a telltale mine as it advances. When fully grown – about 0.15 in (4 mm) long – it either chews its way out of the leaf or drops to the ground when the leaf falls. Once on the ground, it completes its development, turning into a tiny moth.

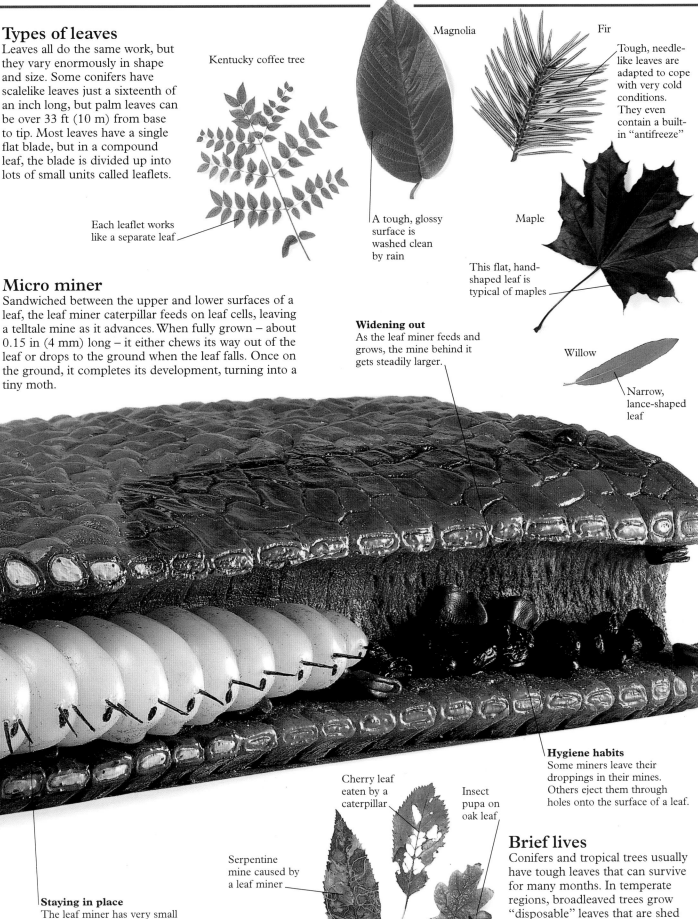

Widening out
As the leaf miner feeds and grows, the mine behind it gets steadily larger.

Hygiene habits
Some miners leave their droppings in their mines. Others eject them through holes onto the surface of a leaf.

Staying in place
The leaf miner has very small legs. Sideways-pointing bristles help to anchor it while it feeds.

Serpentine mine caused by a leaf miner

Cherry leaf eaten by a caterpillar

Insect pupa on oak leaf

Brief lives

Conifers and tropical trees usually have tough leaves that can survive for many months. In temperate regions, broadleaved trees grow "disposable" leaves that are shed every year. These leaves are often attacked by leaf miners and other small animals.

13

Beneath the bark

Bark beetle

W ood is one of the toughest materials in the plant world – it has to be to enable trees to stay upright. But despite its great strength, wood is produced almost entirely by a single, wafer-thin layer of living cells. This layer, called the vascular cambium, is hidden safely beneath the bark. Every year it undergoes a burst of growth, producing a new layer of wood. At the same time, the bark also grows and expands, ensuring that the soft new wood is protected from the outside world. The result – after many years – is layer upon layer of wood, and a strong thick trunk that supports the branches of a fully grown tree.

Living layers

In this tree, the layers of bark and wood have been peeled back to show how the trunk is made up. The tree's cells form distinct layers, and each layer has its own function. Each year, the cambium layer produces xylem cells, which form an annual ring. In dry years, the rings are narrower than in wet years. When a tree has been cut down, it is possible to tell how old it is by the number of rings there are in the trunk.

Peeling bark

Like most eucalyptuses or gum trees, the cider gum has outer bark that peels away in long vertical strips. The bark is creamy white when freshly exposed, becoming darker with age.

Cork

Cork oaks have unusually thick outer bark that can be stripped away without harming the tree. It is used for corking bottles and making cork tiles.

Papery bark

The bark of birch trees is particularly durable and often peels away in thin, curling sheets. In some parts of the world, birch bark was once used as a form of paper.

Outer bark
This part of the bark consists entirely of dead cells. It protects the tree against heat and cold, and also makes it more difficult for animals to get at the living wood.

Inner bark
Also known as the phloem, this layer of cells carries sap up and down the tree. Because sap is full of nutritious sugar, the inner bark is often attacked by wood-boring insects such as bark beetles, which bore patterned tunnels, called galleries, into the wood.

Vascular cambium
This layer is just a few cells thick. When the cells divide, they produce new phloem cells, and new wood (xylem) cells. Like the other layers, the cambium covers the entire surface of the tree, including every branch and twig.

Sapwood
Sapwood consists of living xylem cells. These cells carry water and are very tough, giving the wood its strength.

Heartwood
As xylem cells become older, they gradually lose their ability to carry water. They also become packed with resins and other chemicals, protecting them from insects and invading fungi. Eventually the cells die, becoming heartwood – the hardest part of the tree.

Fire protection
The world's heaviest tree is the giant sequoia, a native of California. It has spongy, fibrous bark that can be over 1 ft (30 cm) thick. This bark works like natural fireproofing, allowing the tree to survive summer fires.

Rooted to the spot

Roots anchor trees in the ground and enable water and minerals to be absorbed from the soil. In dry places, roots sometimes extend more than 246 ft (75 m) deep as they search for water, but in most forests they stay much closer to the surface. The roots of mountainside trees grow around boulders and through cracks in rocks, and in tropical rainforests roots often crisscross the ground like fat, overlapping snakes. Some tropical trees, called mangroves, have very unusual roots. These trees live on thick coastal mud, which is flooded twice a day by the incoming tide. A mangrove's roots spread out like a set of sturdy props, keeping the tree securely anchored as the mud gently swirls about below.

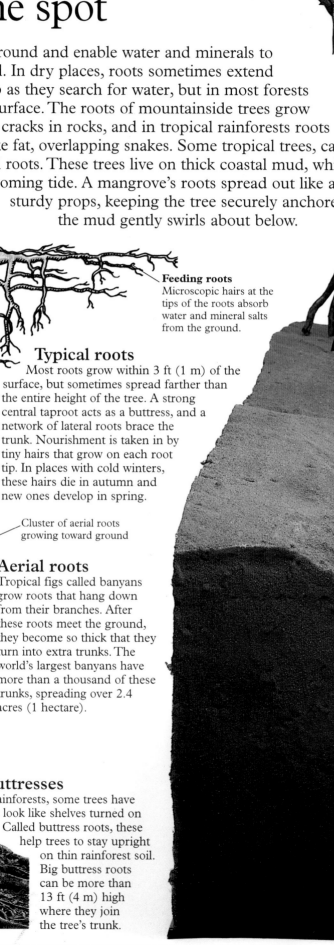

Feeding roots
Microscopic hairs at the tips of the roots absorb water and mineral salts from the ground.

Lateral roots
The lateral roots spread out close to the surface, through the fertile soil layer.

Taproots
The taproot is the anchor of the tree. Taproots are found in many trees, but not in palms.

Typical roots
Most roots grow within 3 ft (1 m) of the surface, but sometimes spread farther than the entire height of the tree. A strong central taproot acts as a buttress, and a network of lateral roots brace the trunk. Nourishment is taken in by tiny hairs that grow on each root tip. In places with cold winters, these hairs die in autumn and new ones develop in spring.

Cluster of aerial roots growing toward ground

Aerial roots
Tropical figs called banyans grow roots that hang down from their branches. After these roots meet the ground, they become so thick that they turn into extra trunks. The world's largest banyans have more than a thousand of these trunks, spreading over 2.4 acres (1 hectare).

Living buttresses
In tropical rainforests, some trees have roots that look like shelves turned on end. Called buttress roots, these help trees to stay upright on thin rainforest soil. Big buttress roots can be more than 13 ft (4 m) high where they join the tree's trunk.

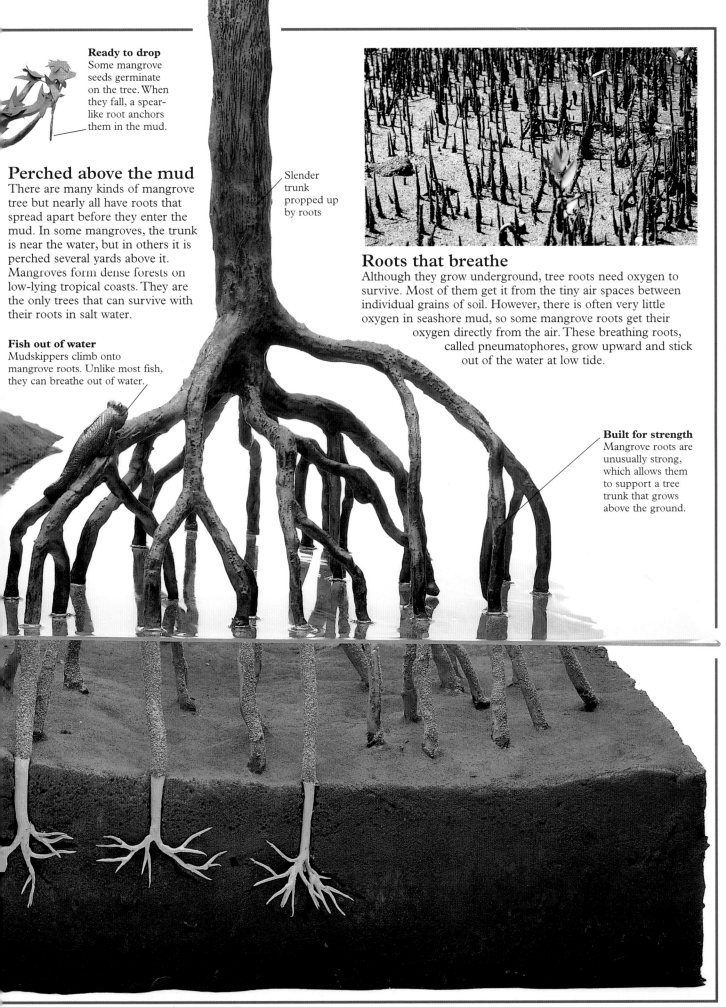

Ready to drop
Some mangrove
seeds germinate
on the tree. When
they fall, a spear-
like root anchors
them in the mud.

Perched above the mud

There are many kinds of mangrove
tree but nearly all have roots that
spread apart before they enter the
mud. In some mangroves, the trunk
is near the water, but in others it is
perched several yards above it.
Mangroves form dense forests on
low-lying tropical coasts. They are
the only trees that can survive with
their roots in salt water.

Fish out of water
Mudskippers climb onto
mangrove roots. Unlike most fish,
they can breathe out of water.

Slender
trunk
propped up
by roots

Roots that breathe

Although they grow underground, tree roots need oxygen to
survive. Most of them get it from the tiny air spaces between
individual grains of soil. However, there is often very little
oxygen in seashore mud, so some mangrove roots get their
oxygen directly from the air. These breathing roots,
called pneumatophores, grow upward and stick
out of the water at low tide.

Built for strength
Mangrove roots are
unusually strong,
which allows them
to support a tree
trunk that grows
above the ground.

17

Pollen dispersal

High up in the branches of a tropical tree, a tiny female wasp crawls through a hole in a young fig and disappears from view. Her journey began on a nearby tree, and she is on a mission to lay her eggs. As well as ensuring that her own young have somewhere safe to live and feed, the fig wasp does something else: she spreads pollen, enabling fig trees to make seeds. The wasps cannot breed without the figs, and the figs cannot make seeds without the wasps. This partnership between figs and wasps is just one example of the way trees manage to scatter pollen so that they can reproduce. Like figs, many trees spread their pollen with the help of insects or animals. Others use the wind to blow their pollen far and wide.

Liquid meal
As it drinks nectar from a banana flower, a bat is dusted with pollen.

Night shift
In tropical forests, many plants are pollinated by bats. Their flowers are usually large and smelly, and they produce lots of sugary nectar. Flowers that are pollinated by bats usually hang away from the leaves, so that bats can hover near them without damaging their wings.

Drifting on the wind
Alder catkins shed clouds of pollen into the air, and the pollen is blown away by the wind. A single catkin releases thousands of pollen grains, but each grain has only a tiny chance of settling on a female flower. Wind pollination is common in forests in cool places, where there are few pollinating insects.

Hidden blooms
A fig's flowers are tiny and packed inside the fleshy, fruitlike case.

Tight squeeze
The entrance is very narrow, and the female wasp sometimes loses her wings as she squeezes through it.

Fruiting fig
There are over 2000 species of figs, growing mainly in the tropics. Each type is pollinated by a different breed of fig wasp. When figs are ripe, they are often eaten by birds, and the seeds pass through their bodies unharmed.

1 All fig wasps grow up inside figs, but only the females have wings. After mating, the females leave the fig, collecting pollen as they crawl out. They fly off to find new figs where they can lay their eggs, carrying the pollen with them.

Guarded entrance
Overlapping scales make it difficult for any other creature to get inside the fig.

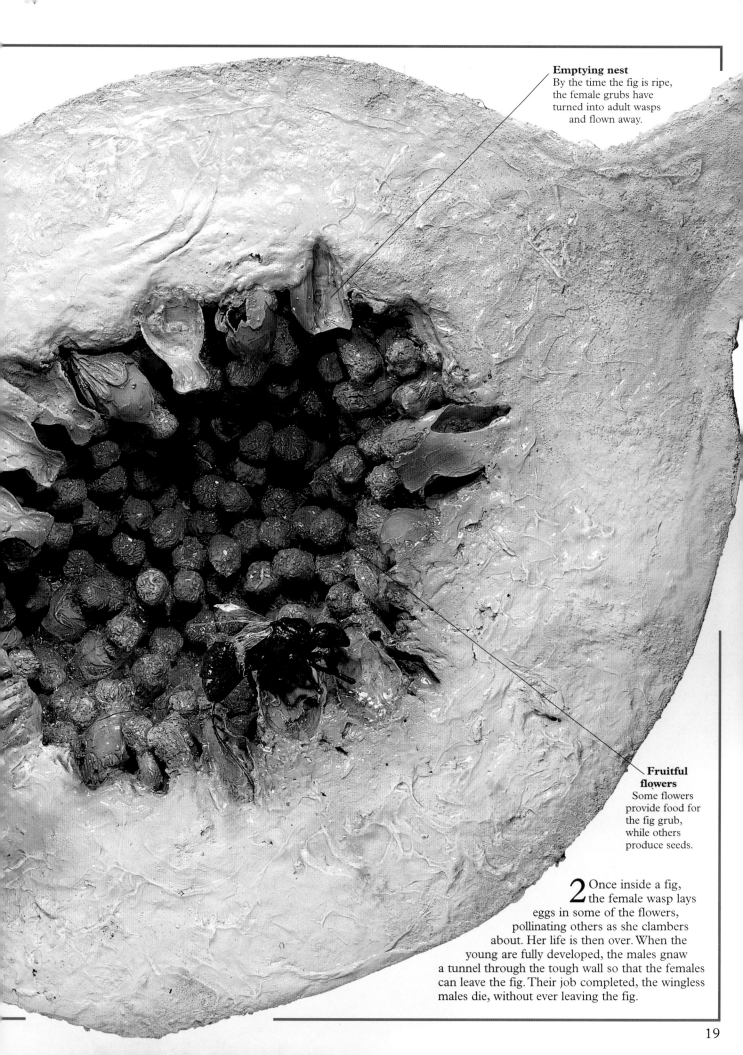

Emptying nest
By the time the fig is ripe,
the female grubs have
turned into adult wasps
and flown away.

**Fruitful
flowers**
Some flowers
provide food for
the fig grub,
while others
produce seeds.

2 Once inside a fig,
the female wasp lays
eggs in some of the flowers,
pollinating others as she clambers
about. Her life is then over. When the
young are fully developed, the males gnaw
a tunnel through the tough wall so that the females
can leave the fig. Their job completed, the wingless
males die, without ever leaving the fig.

Making seeds

Once a tree has been pollinated, it can start to make its seeds. Tree seeds develop in two different ways. Conifers, such as pines and firs, make their seeds on the surface of special scales, which are packed together to form cones. Broadleaved trees do not have cones; instead their seeds develop inside protective chambers called ovaries. Together, an ovary and its seeds make up a fruit. Cones shed their seeds when they are ripe, but many fruits are designed to come away from trees with their seeds still aboard. Fleshy fruits are often eaten by animals, which help to spread the seeds. Dry fruits are often scattered by the wind.

Female cones
The female cones are pollinated soon after they appear, when they are still small and soft.

Young leaves with protective sheaths

Prickly protection
Sweet chestnuts develop inside a prickly case, which helps to protect them from animals as they develop. When the nuts are ripe, the case splits open and the nuts fall to the ground. Many get eaten, but enough survive to produce new trees.

Prickly case containing 2 or 3 nuts

Male cones
Columns of small male cones develop near the ends of the branches in late spring. After shedding clouds of bright yellow pollen, they wither away.

One-year-old cone
By the time a year has passed, the female cones are green and about the size of an egg.

Giant seed
The coco-de-mer is a palm that grows on the Seychelles Islands, in the Indian Ocean. It produces the world's largest seeds, weighing up to 44 lb (20 kg). Each of these gigantic "double coconuts" can take 10 years to develop, and the trees do not begin fruiting until they are at least 25 years old.

Separate sexes
Most trees have male and female flowers, but in some species – such as pistachios and coco-de-mer palms – the male and female flowers grow on separate trees. The female trees produce seeds, but only if a male tree is nearby to pollinate them.

The cone's seeds have just started to develop

Spinning seeds

Sycamores and maples grow their seeds in pairs. Each seed is attached to a wing, so the paired seeds often spin to the ground like miniature helicopters. If the weather is windy enough, the seeds will be spread over a large area.

Seed

Flower stalk

Extension of fruit wall forms a wing

Fruit wall protecting seed

Paired leaves
Scots pine leaves grow in pairs and last for several years.

Ash keys

A single ash tree can produce up to 100,000 winged seeds – known as "keys" – every year. Some of the seeds germinate as soon as they reach the ground, but most do not grow for one or two years. Ash trees use the wind to pollinate their flowers and to spread their seeds.

Leaving home
Each seed has a thin, papery wing that helps to carry it away from the parent tree.

Shedding seeds
Warm sunshine dries out the scales and makes them fold back. The ripe seeds are now ready to flutter to the ground.

Seeds in cones

The Scots pine has male and female cones that grow on the same tree. The male cones wither away soon after they have released their pollen, but the female cones last much longer, turning brown and woody as they get older. Eventually their scales open, releasing the seeds.

Mature cones
The female cones ripen in their third year. By now, their scales are tough and woody.

Main bud at tip of branch
grows faster than the other buds

Paired side buds

Branch
produced by
a side bud
from the
previous
year

Bursting buds

In parts of the world where it is always warm and wet, trees can grow year round. But in places that have cold winters, most trees stop growing for several months a year. While they are dormant, these trees often seem dead, but as spring arrives they suddenly change. Millions of buds burst open, and the trees start growing once again. Buds are miniature shoots, packed inside cases made of hard scales. The scales protect the inside of the bud from the cold and from drying winds. When the weather warms up, the scales fold back and the stem inside begins to grow. Within a few days, the bare branches are covered in a haze of green as the tree starts coming into leaf.

Pole position

In many trees – like this horse chestnut – the biggest buds are always at the end of the branches. Side buds farther back can take the place of the main bud if it is broken off.

Inside a bud

A bud contains a complete shoot hidden away from the outside world. The shoot is embryonic, meaning that it is still at an early stage of development. Most buds start to form in midsummer – long before the cold weather begins. By the time winter arrives, they are fully formed and ready to cope with cold winds and frost.

Side buds

Growth hormones from the main bud make sure that the side buds grow more slowly than it does. If this did not happen, the tree would grow out of shape.

Hidden leaves
Embryonic leaves are packed tightly together around the center of the bud, helping to keep it warm.

Growing point
This small area at the center of the bud is called the meristem. It contains cells that divide very rapidly when the bud bursts and starts to grow.

Spaced apart
The space between buds is called an internode. On some fast-growing stems, each internode can be over 20 in (50 cm) long.

Special chemicals
Chemicals in the bud scales help to prevent the shoot growing during the winter.

Leaf scar
This scar was left by a leaf breaking off.

Feeding on buds

During the winter, buds provide some animals with a much-needed source of food. In Europe and northern Asia, the bullfinch often feeds on fruit tree buds, making this handsome bird unpopular with farmers and gardeners.

Weatherproof skin
The bud scales have a waterproof coat that prevents the interior of the bud from getting either too damp or too dry.

1 During the winter, the bud is tightly closed. In most buds, the shoot inside cannot start to grow until it has experienced several weeks of cold weather. This keeps the bud from bursting at the wrong time – for example during short spells of mild weather before winter is truly over.

Unrolling fronds

Tree ferns grow in moist places, often under the shade of larger trees. Instead of bursting out of buds, their feathery fronds grow by slowly unrolling. In some tree ferns, many fronds unroll at the same time, and each one can be up to 16 ft (5 m) long when it is fully grown.

Wet and dry

This cluster of young leaves belongs to a plant called a cycad. Cycads look like palm trees, but they evolved millions of years before palms first appeared. Most cycads live in places that have a wet season and a dry season, rather than winter and summer. Trees in these places usually start to grow when the wet season begins.

Burst of growth
A cycad's tough leaves may last for several years.

Breathing free
Freed of their covering of scales, the leaves can start to collect carbon dioxide from the air.

Soaking up the sun
Young leaves spread apart and expand to absorb as much sunlight as possible.

Water on the move
Water starts to evaporate from the young leaves as they draw more water up from the tree's roots.

Job done
The bud scales slowly shrivel up and eventually fall away from the branch.

Folding back
The bud scales hinge backward and begin to dry out.

2 As the days get longer in early spring, the bud starts to stir into life. Cells inside the shoot begin to divide, and the bud scales slowly fold back. As soon as the weather starts to warm up, the bud's prepacked leaves begin to grow, the shoot lengthens, and the bud bursts open.

3 By now the leaves have grown clear of the bud and can start the urgent task of gathering light. At this time of the year, the days are lengthening rapidly, even though the weather sometimes turns cold. For a few weeks, the shoot may grow by up to 1 in (2.5 cm) a day – as fast as some trees grow in some tropical forests.

Sticky situations

For any tree, being injured can have dangerous results. If one of its branches is torn off by the wind, or if an animal chews into its bark, insects and fungi may be able to attack the wood inside. To reduce the chances of this happening, trees have special fluids that seal up wounds and keep animals at bay. The stickiest of these is resin; a molasseslike substance made by conifers and some other trees. Resin is liquid when it first oozes out of a tree, but it slowly dries to form a hard patch that seals the wound. Another of these liquids is latex. Unlike resin, latex is milky white and contains a cocktail of powerful chemicals that gives it a burning taste.

Amber
This fossilized resin, called amber, contains a trapped insect.

Harvesting latex
These rubber trees have had grooves cut into their bark to make them drip latex, which is collected in a cup. The latex from these trees is dried and used to make natural rubber.

Sap stealers
These strange creatures are female scale insects. While the males of the species fly from tree to tree, the wingless females spend their lives in one place drinking sap. Unlike resin, sap is normally kept locked away beneath a tree's bark, and the scale insects have to use piercing mouthparts to get at their liquid food.

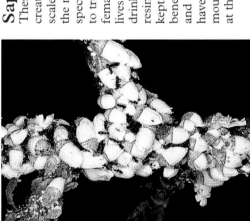

Feeding on gum
Instead of resin, many trees seal wounds with sugary gum. Some forest mammals specialize in eating gum and have digestive systems that are modified to deal with this unusual kind of food. In South America, marmosets start the gum flowing by biting chunks out of a tree's bark.

Tapping in
A marmoset gouges holes in the bark with its lower front teeth.

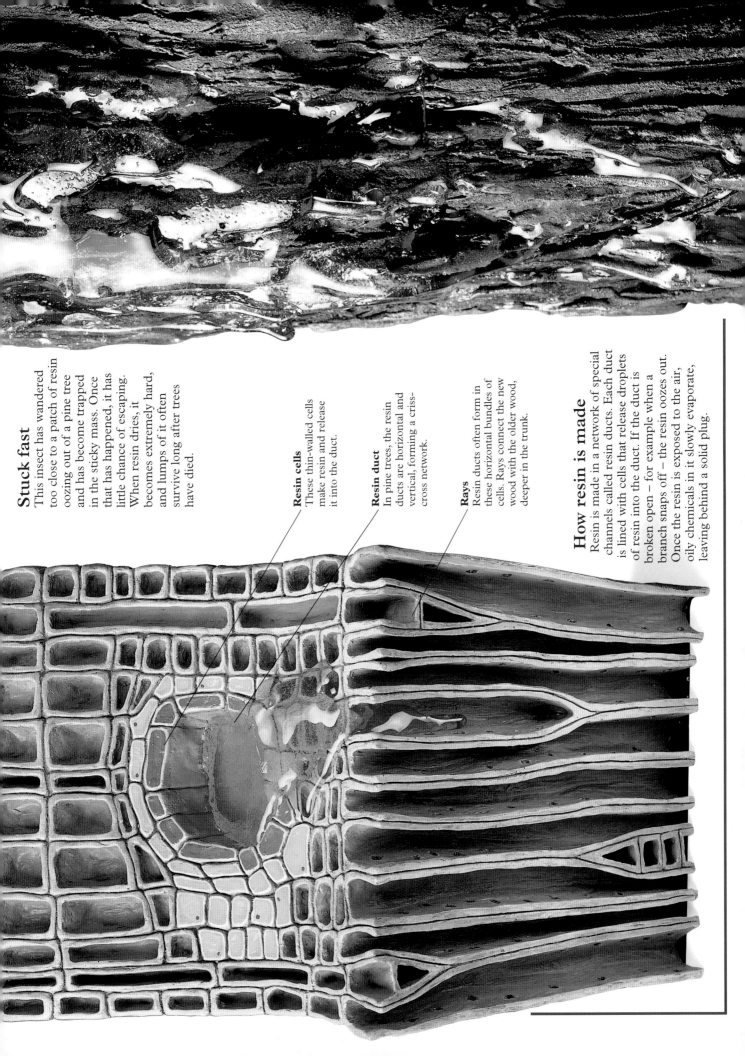

Stuck fast

This insect has wandered too close to a patch of resin oozing out of a pine tree and has become trapped in the sticky mass. Once that has happened, it has little chance of escaping. When resin dries, it becomes extremely hard, and lumps of it often survive long after trees have died.

Resin cells
These thin-walled cells make resin and release it into the duct.

Resin duct
In pine trees, the resin ducts are horizontal and vertical, forming a criss-cross network.

Rays
Resin ducts often form in these horizontal bundles of cells. Rays connect the new wood with the older wood, deeper in the trunk.

How resin is made

Resin is made in a network of special channels called resin ducts. Each duct is lined with cells that release droplets of resin into the duct. If the duct is broken open – for example when a branch snaps off – the resin oozes out. Once the resin is exposed to the air, oily chemicals in it slowly evaporate, leaving behind a solid plug.

Self-defense

If an animal tries to eat the leaves of a bull's-horn acacia, it gets an unpleasant surprise. Within seconds, hundreds of ants pour out of the tree's hollow thorns and vigorously defend the tree. Although the ants are small, they have painful bites and stings, and soon the attacker is on the retreat. This remarkable partnership between ants and acacias is just one example of the ways trees defend themselves. Many other trees have poisonous leaves or thorns and spines that make them difficult to eat. Like the acacia's ants, these defenses give them the best chances in the struggle for a share of the forest.

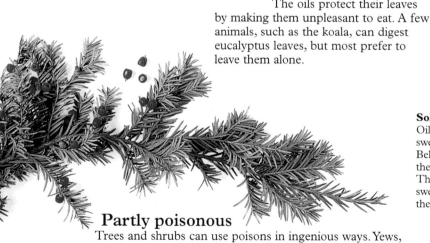

Dangerous seeds

Laburnums need to keep hungry animals away from their developing seeds. They do this by using chemical weapons – poisonous substances that are stored in every seed.

Spearlike spines

Sharp spines protect holly leaves from deer and other forest animals. In most holly trees, only the lowest leaves are spiny. The ones higher up, which are safely out of reach, are often smooth.

Odorous oils

Gum trees, or eucalyptuses, are packed with strong-smelling oils. The oils protect their leaves by making them unpleasant to eat. A few animals, such as the koala, can digest eucalyptus leaves, but most prefer to leave them alone.

On patrol

At any time, about a quarter of the ant colony is on patrol. The ants attack any animals that try to graze the tree. They also prune away any plants, such as vines, that attempt to grow on their host.

Solid food

Oily, protein-rich swellings, called Beltian bodies, grow at the tips of the leaflets. The ants harvest these swellings and feed them to their grubs.

Partly poisonous

Trees and shrubs can use poisons in ingenious ways. Yews, for example, have poisonous leaves and seeds, but their bright red "berries" are a tasty food for birds. The birds digest the berries but not the seeds, which are scattered in their droppings. In this way, yews protect themselves against grazers, while ensuring that their seeds are still distributed by birds.

Unfettered growth

Bull's-horn acacias grow in the forests of Central America. The acacia's ants fend off the climbing plants that threaten to smother the saplings, allowing them to grow up to their full height of 66 ft (20 m).

Worker ant
Workers feed the queen and carry her eggs to other thorns where the ant grubs develop. The ant colony eventually occupies all the thorns on the tree.

Thorns growing at the base of a compound leaf

Liquid food
Special nectaries at the base of each leaf provide the ants with sugar-rich nectar.

Queen ant
The ant colony is founded by a single queen ant. She flies to a young acacia tree, chews her way into one of its thorns, and starts laying eggs. Her body becomes so big that she cannot crawl out of the thorn.

Hidden home
The ants cut an entrance hole in each thorn. They then chew away the soft interior to make a hollow chamber.

Live-in partners

Ants make a home in an acacia when the tree is still very young. They live inside the tree's thorns and feed on food that the tree produces for them. In return for this food, the ants defend their tree against attack. The ants depend on the acacias for their survival. The acacias can survive without their ants, but they do not grow as well.

Bark busters

Bark is like a tree's skin. It stops the trunk from drying out and helps to protect the wood from hungry wildlife. Most forest animals cannot break open this tough barrier, but a handful are not so easily deterred. These are the bark busters – animals that are specially equipped to get through the bark and into the living wood beneath. Woodpeckers are the greatest experts at this kind of work. Using their chisel-like beaks, they excavate holes as they search for insect grubs. Squirrels and other mammals gnaw through the bark with their teeth to feed on newly formed wood. Unlike woodpeckers, they usually do this only when other food is hard to find.

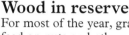

Stripped branches often die

Wood in reserve
For most of the year, gray squirrels feed on nuts and other seeds. They store food for the winter, but in early spring, their stores often begin to run out. New wood is the squirrels' emergency food. In order to survive the lean months, they tear strips of bark from branches to get at the sap-rich wood underneath.

Porcupine's favorite
Spruce trees, which often grow in mountainous forests, are especially vulnerable to porcupine damage.

Damaged by deer
Deer can cause a lot of damage to trees, particularly in cold winter weather. This beech tree has been gnawed by red deer, leaving a large wound in its trunk. Large trees can recover from this kind of damage, but for small saplings, deer damage often proves fatal.

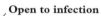

Open to infection
Damaged bark can allow fungal spores to settle on living wood, infecting the tree.

Gnawing teeth
The North American porcupine is a good climber and often feeds high above the ground. Like a squirrel, it has two pairs of extra-large, bright orange front teeth, which it uses to gnaw through bark. These grow continuously, keeping them from wearing out.

Big head
Moose antlers can measure nearly 6 ft (2 m) from tip to tip.

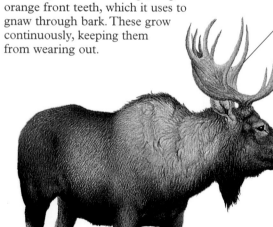

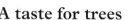
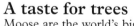

A taste for trees
Moose are the world's biggest deer. A fully grown male can eat 44 lb (20 kg) of food a day and, in the winter, most of this consists of bark and leaves. Its overhanging top lip enables the moose to tear off leaves and branches easily. To get at the higher branches, a moose will sometimes bend small trees over until they snap in two.

Smash-and-grab

Woodpeckers are unusual birds in many ways. They have extremely tough beaks and strong neck muscles, and remarkably long tongues that often have a spiny or sticky tip. The greater spotted woodpecker, shown here, hacks open bark to feed on insect grubs. Larger woodpeckers often chisel into trees to eat the young of other birds.

Shock absorber
A woodpecker's skull and brain are built to withstand the sudden impact as it smashes its way through the bark. Most birds would be knocked out by this method of feeding.

Feeling the way
The woodpecker's tongue snakes its way along the tunnel made by a wood-boring grub. With a quick flick, the grub is pulled out of its tunnel and swallowed whole.

Pine parasite

During the height of summer, pine woods teem with insect life. Many of these insects feed on pine needles or wood, but ichneumon flies have a more sinister way of life. Ichneumons start life as grubs that feed on other insects. In pine woods, adult females flutter from tree to tree, using their remarkable sense of smell to find insect larvae hidden deep inside the wood. When an ichneumon locates a larva, she bores through the wood with a special tube and lays a single egg in or beside it. When the ichneumon hatches, it uses the larva as a living source of food.

Living drill

This ichneumon fly, called *Rhyssa persuasoria*, lays its eggs on wood-boring sawfly grubs. Once the ichneumon has located a suitable grub, she grips the bark with her feet, and drills down toward it with a special ovipositor (egg-laying tube) that is nearly 2 in (5 cm) long. She lays a single egg, before flying away to find another victim.

Ovipositor sheath
This long case protects the ovipositor when it is not being used.

Bent double
The ichneumon bends her slender abdomen so that she can drill into the wood underneath her body.

Slow work
It can take up to 30 minutes for the ichneumon to drill its way through the wood to the sawfly grub.

Cutting tool
The ovipositor is thinner than a human hair, with a sharp tip. The ichneumon twists her abdomen one way and then the other so that her ovipositor cuts through the wood.

Bark-eating weevil

The pine weevil feeds on the bark of young pine shoots. This insect can be a serious pest in pine plantations, because it can stop new shoots growing normally. Pine weevils spend the first part of their lives as larvae hidden inside roots and tree stumps.

Rostrum
The weevil has sharp, biting jaws at the end of a long snout, or rostrum.

"Elbowed" antenna

Chemical clue
The ichneumon uses its antennae to locate a microscopic fungus that grows in the sawfly grub's tunnels.

Out in the open

Unlike sawfly larvae that bore into wood, the larvae of the pine sawfly feed in the open. They eat pine needles, chewing them up with their tough jaws. If the larvae are threatened by a predator, such as a bird, they wave their bodies around to make themselves look dangerous.

Sitting duck
Sawfly grubs have tiny legs and are too slow to escape when the ichneumon drills toward them.

Turning the tables
Resin normally keeps insects at bay, but resin-gall caterpillars use it for their own protection.

Resin home

The resin-gall moth lays its eggs on young pine shoots, and its caterpillars chew their way into the wood. The tree oozes sticky resin, which eventually forms a hard lump. The caterpillars use this lump of resin as a winter home, safe from the cold weather and from hungry birds.

Taking to the air
The caterpillars gnaw out of the resin hideaway in spring and then turn into adult moths.

Strangler fig

High up in a tropical tree, a sapling germinates in the fork of a branch. The leafy hitchhiker looks harmless but it is far more dangerous than it appears. The sapling is a strangler fig and, as the years go by, will turn into an unyielding killer. Strangler figs use other trees to give them a head start in the struggle for light. Their seeds are carried by fruit-eating birds, which shed them in their sticky droppings. At first, a young strangler fig is too small to cause any trouble, but once its roots make contact with the ground, things soon begin to change. The strangler starts to outgrow its host, engulfing it in a living coffin of interlocking roots.

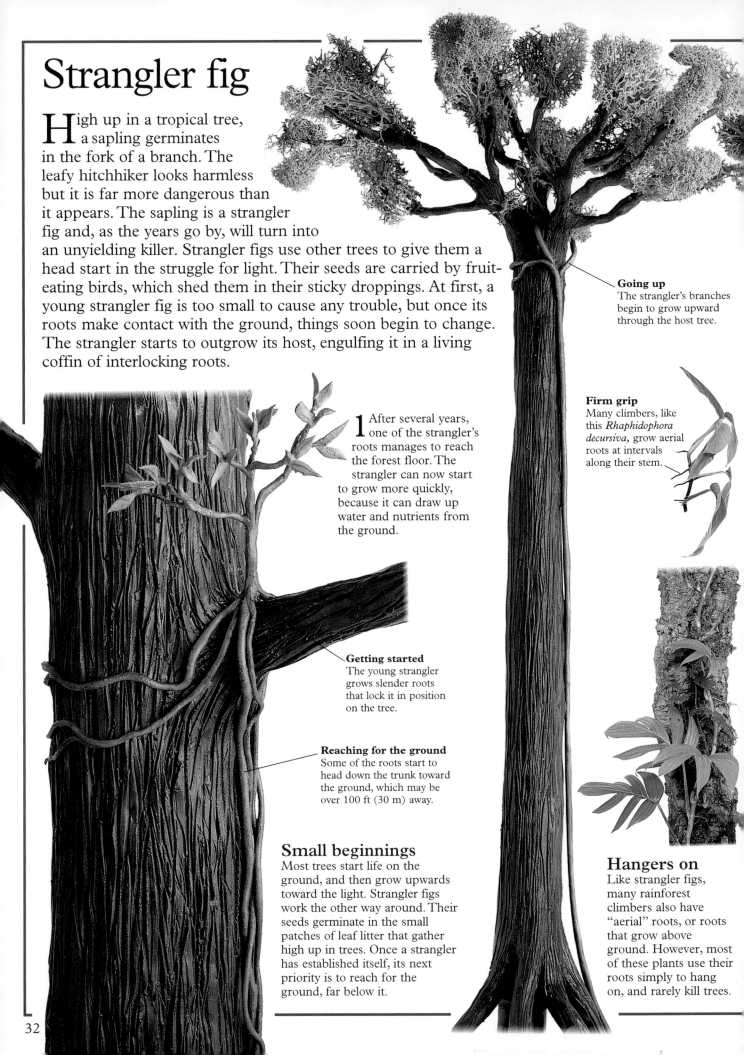

Going up
The strangler's branches begin to grow upward through the host tree.

Firm grip
Many climbers, like this *Rhaphidophora decursiva*, grow aerial roots at intervals along their stem.

1 After several years, one of the strangler's roots manages to reach the forest floor. The strangler can now start to grow more quickly, because it can draw up water and nutrients from the ground.

Getting started
The young strangler grows slender roots that lock it in position on the tree.

Reaching for the ground
Some of the roots start to head down the trunk toward the ground, which may be over 100 ft (30 m) away.

Small beginnings
Most trees start life on the ground, and then grow upwards toward the light. Strangler figs work the other way around. Their seeds germinate in the small patches of leaf litter that gather high up in trees. Once a strangler has established itself, its next priority is to reach for the ground, far below it.

Hangers on
Like strangler figs, many rainforest climbers also have "aerial" roots, or roots that grow above ground. However, most of these plants use their roots simply to hang on, and rarely kill trees.

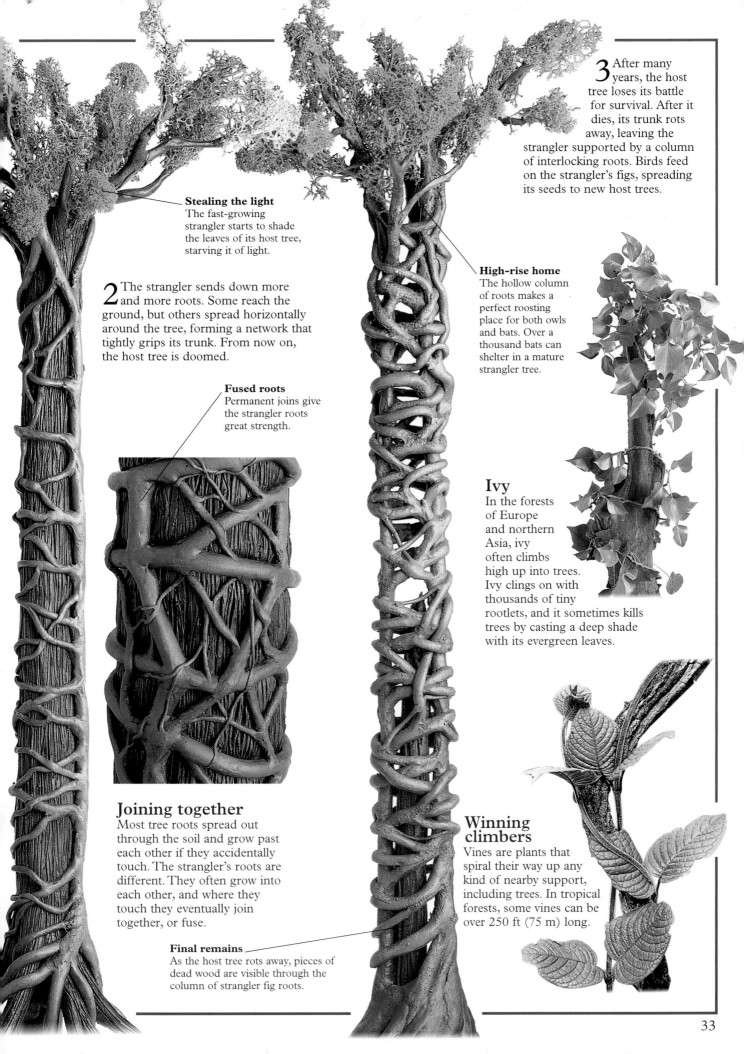

3 After many years, the host tree loses its battle for survival. After it dies, its trunk rots away, leaving the strangler supported by a column of interlocking roots. Birds feed on the strangler's figs, spreading its seeds to new host trees.

Stealing the light
The fast-growing strangler starts to shade the leaves of its host tree, starving it of light.

2 The strangler sends down more and more roots. Some reach the ground, but others spread horizontally around the tree, forming a network that tightly grips its trunk. From now on, the host tree is doomed.

High-rise home
The hollow column of roots makes a perfect roosting place for both owls and bats. Over a thousand bats can shelter in a mature strangler tree.

Fused roots
Permanent joins give the strangler roots great strength.

Ivy

In the forests of Europe and northern Asia, ivy often climbs high up into trees. Ivy clings on with thousands of tiny rootlets, and it sometimes kills trees by casting a deep shade with its evergreen leaves.

Joining together

Most tree roots spread out through the soil and grow past each other if they accidentally touch. The strangler's roots are different. They often grow into each other, and where they touch they eventually join together, or fuse.

Winning climbers

Vines are plants that spiral their way up any kind of nearby support, including trees. In tropical forests, some vines can be over 250 ft (75 m) long.

Final remains
As the host tree rots away, pieces of dead wood are visible through the column of strangler fig roots.

33

Fungus attack

Forests teem with fungi. Their slender feeding threads probe their way through the ground, searching out anything that they can digest, while their microscopic spores drift through the air, settling on leaves, fallen logs, and living wood. If just one of these threads or spores manages to break through a tree's defenses, the fungus can start to feed and may eventually kill the tree. Fungi kill more trees than anything else in forests, but despite this, not all fungi are harmful. Many trees actually depend on fungi to help them extract nutrients from the soil. Without their hidden underground partners, these trees would find it much harder to survive.

Yellow death

Honey fungus is one of the most deadly enemies of trees. Its yellow toadstools release spores that often germinate on rotting tree stumps. Once the fungus has become established, it sends out black underground strands called rhizomorphs. If a rhizomorph makes contact with a tree root, it grows up it and attacks the tree.

Tangled strands of rhizomorphs clearly visible beneath the bark

Feeding on cones

The honey fungus attacks the wood of all kinds of trees, but many fungi are much more particular about their food. These slender toadstools have been produced by a fungus that lives only on the fallen cones of spruce trees.

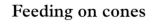

Friendly fungus

The fly agaric fungus produces colorful but poisonous toadstools. They nearly always grow near birch trees or conifers, because the fungus forms partnerships with these particular trees. The fungus helps the trees to absorb nutrients from the soil, while the trees supply the fungus with a little of the food that they make.

Moving on

Near the base of the tree, fungal strands grow away from the tree trunk and into the earth. They spread through the soil, seeking other trees to infect.

Death of a tree
Beneath the bark of an infected tree, honey fungus strands, or rhizomorphs, run like railroad lines up the trunk. The rhizomorphs produce feeding threads that attack living wood, killing the cells that the tree needs to grow. Honey fungus strands are unusually thick and tough. They have even been known to break into drainpipes buried in the ground.

Making spores
Each toadstool makes spores on flaps called gills. Unlike the fungus's strands, spores can be blown by the wind to infect trees far away.

Glowing in the dark
Some fungi – including the honey fungus – have feeding threads and toadstools that glow in the dark. The light that they produce is usually bluish green. Luminous toadstools may help to attract insects that spread spores, but no one knows why feeding threads also glow.

Staying dry
The fungus's toadstools are made of tightly packed microscopic threads. The cap prevents the spores from getting wet when it rains.

Fertile fruit
Each yellow fruiting body releases thousands of tiny spores.

Spreading upward
The fungal strands grow through the tree's vascular cambium – the thin sheet of cells that divide to form new wood.

Recycling remains
Fungi that feed on dead wood perform a valuable service for trees. By breaking down the wood, they release its nutrients back into the soil. This piece of dead wood is covered by the fruiting bodies of the lemon disk fungus, which usually grows on fallen branches that have lost their bark.

Canopy life

For the inhabitants of the rainforest canopy, the ground can be an alien place. Surrounded by a sea of sunlit leaves, many never need any contact with the forest floor far below. The most numerous of these canopy-dwellers are epiphytes – plants that use trees as living perches in their search for light. In some forests, every branch is crammed with these plant passengers, making gardens in the sky. Epiphytes get the nutrients they need from decaying leaves, but finding enough water can be difficult. Bromeliads solve this problem by having a private water tank. Each tank is a miniature habitat for animal life.

Tree boa
This snake is a canopy predator.

Careful parents
Most poison-arrow frogs live on the forest floor, but some carry their tadpoles up to bromeliad pools to protect them from danger. In some species, the adult females visit their tadpoles and feed them with special eggs.

High-rise nursery
Bromeliad pools make ideal breeding grounds for mosquitoes. Adult mosquitoes lay their eggs in the pool, and the eggs hatch into wriggling larvae. The larvae feed on microscopic animals.

Climbers and passengers
In tropical rainforests, many plants scramble up trees to get a share of the light. However, unlike these climbers, epiphytes spend their whole lives off the ground. Some epiphytes have sticky seeds that are spread by canopy animals. Others, such as orchids, have dustlike seeds that are spread over the canopy by the wind.

Mosquito larvae

Absorbing nutrients
Different types of epiphytes share this branch. Their roots absorb nutrients from plant debris that builds up on the branch.

Collecting rain
Each time it rains, the leaves channel rainwater toward the center of the plant, filling its water store.

Leaf life cycle
Each leaf begins life in the center of the plant. As it gets older, it is pushed outward. After a year or more, it shrivels and dies.

Visitor from the ground
Opossums are small marsupials (pouched mammals) that live in the forests of Central and South America. They are good climbers and often investigate bromeliads for insects and small animals.

Slow progress
Flatworms live among bromeliad leaves and do not often come out into the open. They glide slowly over the leaves' surfaces, searching for tiny animals or their dead remains.

Carried to water
The tadpoles of poison-arrow frogs reach the bromeliad pool on the back of one of their parents. A special glue fastens the tadpole in place, but dissolves when the tadpole is placed in water.

Bromeliad crabs
These crabs rarely stray from the bromeliad's water tank. The pool even serves as a watery nursery for their young.

Taking a breather
The maggot's breathing tube opens like a telescope to make contact with the surface.

Getting a grip
The bromeliad's roots grow around a branch to lock the plant in place.

Rat-tailed maggot
Rat-tailed maggots are the larvae of hoverflies, which feed on nectar and pollen from flowers. The larvae grow up in water, and they breathe through a tube that works like a snorkel.

Storing water
Bromeliads are tropical plants that grow in Central and South America. Some live on the ground, but many perch on the branches of trees. In species called tank bromeliads, the plant's leaves overlap to form a watertight central reservoir. A big tank bromeliad can be over 3 ft (1 m) across and may hold several gallons of water.

Forest dwellers

A mature tree is like a multistory building, with a host of different residents on each floor. At the lowest level are animals such as badgers and rabbits, which burrow beneath the tree, using its roots as ready-made supports. Above them in the tree's trunk, birds set up home in cavities in the wood. Woodpeckers excavate holes themselves, but most other birds either take over old woodpecker holes or move into hollows where the wood has started to rot. The tree's branches provide homes for birds and for squirrels, and even its leaves have their own inhabitants. Rolled up to make tiny tubes, they create a snug hideaway for developing beetle grubs.

Home beneath the roots

Badgers often tunnel beneath trees, because tree roots bind the soil together and stop it collapsing. Each network of badger tunnels, called a sett, is used by many generations of animals and can be over 100 years old. As the trees grow and put out new roots, the badgers keep digging new tunnels around them, slowly enlarging the sett.

Collecting bedding
The badger tucks dry grass under its chin and backs into the sett. Badgers keep their sleeping chambers lined with grass and other nesting materials.

Squirrel drey

Squirrels build ball-shaped nests called dreys, usually in the fork of a high branch. The outer part of a drey is made from sticks and leaves. The center is lined with tightly packed dry grass, which helps to keep it warm and weatherproof.

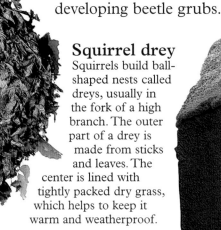

Hidden homes

In forests, dead and dying trees make ideal animal homes, because they often contain cavities that can be used as nests. Like most hole-nesting birds, owls sometimes clean out their homes before laying their eggs, but they rarely bother to line them with any nesting material.

Nocturnal habits
Badgers tend to stay inside the sett during the day, emerging to feed only after dusk.

Open house
Tree holes protect young birds from the weather, but leave them vulnerable to attack by predators.

Badgers' setts often have more than ten entrances

Protected
Leaf tube hides the beetle larva from insect-eating birds.

Rolling a home

The oak leaf roller beetle uses leaves as homes and food for its young. The female chews a line through the blade of a leaf and rolls up part of the leaf to make a tube. She then lays a single egg inside the tube. When the grub hatches, it feeds on the remains of the leaf.

Home improvements
A big sett can have 20 nest chambers and over 1,640 ft (500 m) of tunnels.

Leaf litter

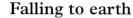

In forests all over the world, a continual cascade of dead leaves tumbles toward the ground. Some trees lose their worn-out leaves throughout the year, but others drop them all at once, shedding hundreds of thousands in just a few weeks. Where do all these leaves go? The answer is that they are broken down by living things, and their nutrients are recycled. In tropical forests, dead leaves are broken down very quickly. In temperate forests, where the climate is cooler, leaves take longer to decay. Here, they often form a deep layer of leaf litter that teems with life.

Falling to earth

Before an oak tree sheds its leaves, it absorbs most of the useful substances that they contain. The leaves' green pigment – chlorophyll – begins to break down, making the leaves turn yellow and then brown. They are then ready to drop.

Fast turnaround

In tropical rainforests, the weather is always warm and wet, and dead leaves break down within days of reaching the ground. As a result, the leaf litter is quite thin. Many rainforest trees grow fine rootlets that fan out across the surface, soaking up nutrients from dead leaves before the rain washes them away.

Predator on patrol
Ground beetles search among the leaves for food. Anything they can overpower is fair game.

Earthy life
Cockchafer larvae live in the soil and feed on tree roots.

Leafy hideout
Earwigs feed at night, eating practically anything they can find. During the day they hide away among the leaves.

Unfussy eaters
Woodlice feed on all kinds of plant remains, including fallen leaves.

Dragged underground
Earthworms sometimes pull leaves beneath the surface so that they can nibble parts of them in the safety of their burrows. By burying leaves, they help to make the soil more fertile.

Essential service
Earthworms' tunnels let the soil "breathe" and help rainwater drain away.

Life in the leaf litter

Leaf litter is packed with living things, but many are so small that they can only be seen with a microscope. However, the giants of the leaf litter world are much easier to spot. They include earthworms, millipedes, and woodlice – which eat the dead remains of leaves and wood – together with fast-moving hunters such as ground beetles and centipedes.

Raining leaves
Up to quarter of a
million leaves may be
shed every autumn by
a mature oak tree.

Old cells
In autumn, cells at the
end of each leaf stalk
become weak, making
the leaf fall off.

Conifer leaf litter
In coniferous forests, the leaf litter can
be very deep, but not many animals live
in it. This is because conifer leaves are
tough and take a long time to break
down. Some ants use the dead leaves
as building material, piling them up
in nests 5 ft (1.5 m) high.

Dead pine leaves
(needles) can take more
than a year to break down

Organic feeder
Millipedes help to
recycle plant remains
by living on a purely
vegetarian diet.

Killing claws
Some centipedes live above
ground, while others stay
below the surface. All live by
hunting and kill their prey by
using poisonous claws near
their heads.

Slime trail
Slugs can only survive
in damp places, and
the woodland floor
suits them well.

Wormcasts
Earthworms eat their
way through the soil,
ejecting the leftovers
in piles called
wormcasts. In this
way, soil from deep
down is mixed with
surface soil.

Glossary

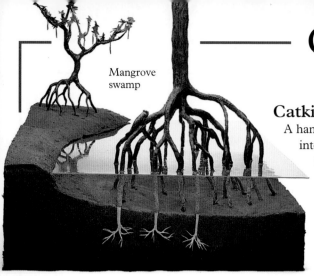

Mangrove swamp

A

Aerial root
A root that grows above the ground. Some trees use aerial roots to prop themselves up, while climbing plants use them to hang on.

B

Broadleaved tree
A tree with broad, flat leaves, such as an oak or maple. All broadleaved trees reproduce by growing flowers.

Bromeliad
A member of a family of plants that grows in warm parts of the Americas. Bromeliads usually have narrow, spiky leaves, and many of them live on trees.

Buttress root
A root that has a tall, vertical flap where it joins a tree's trunk. Buttress roots are common in tropical rainforests, but are rare elsewhere.

C

Cambium
A thin layer of cells beneath the surface of a tree's roots, branches, and trunk. Unlike other cells in a tree, those in the cambium divide and grow every year, producing xylem on one side and phloem on the other side.

Canopy
A layer above the forest floor formed by the interconnecting crowns of trees.

Catkin
A hanging flower that sheds pollen into the air, so that it can drift away in the wind.

Cell
The smallest complete unit of living matter. In trees, most cells have tough walls that give them their strength.

Chlorophyll
The green chemical that plants use when they carry out photosynthesis, to collect the energy in sunlight.

Compound leaf
A leaf that is divided up into many separate parts called leaflets. Hickories and horse chestnuts are examples of trees with compound leaves.

Conifer
A tree or shrub that bears cones to reproduce.

Crown shyness
A way of growing seen in tropical trees that makes each tree "shy away" from its neighbors. As a result, their crowns never touch one another.

Resin duct

Crown
The upper part of a tree, including all its branches and leaves.

Cycad
A tree that looks like a palm, but which grows its seeds in cones. Cycads first appeared over 300 million years ago, making them among the most ancient trees on Earth.

D

Deciduous
A tree that sheds all its leaves each year.

E

Epiphyte
A plant that grows on other plants and uses them as a perch in order to reach the light.

F

Fungus
An organism that absorbs food from other living things, or from their dead remains.

G

Germination
The process in which a new plant starts to grow from a seed or spore.

H

Heartwood
The old wood in the middle of a tree trunk. Heartwood contains chemicals that help to fend off fungi. It is often darker than the wood around it.

I

Internode
The space on a twig between neighboring leaves or buds.

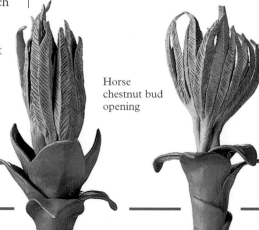

Horse chestnut bud opening

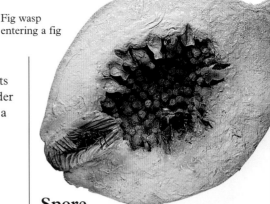

L

Lateral root

A root that grows out sideways from the tree's main tap root, dividing and subdividing near the surface.

Latex

A milky and often poisonous liquid made by some trees and other plants. Trees use latex to prevent animals eating their wood and leaves.

Autumn leaves

M

Meristem

A part of a plant where cells divide rapidly so that the plant can grow. In trees, the fastest-growing meristems are at the tips of the roots and twigs.

N

Nectar

A sugary liquid produced by flowers in order to attract pollinating animals.

O

Ovary

The female part of a tree's flowers that eventually produces seeds.

Ovipositor

A slender tube at the end of an animal's body for laying eggs. In forests, many insects have ovipositors that can pierce leaves or wood to lay eggs inside them.

P

Phloem

A system of microscopic pipelines that trees and other plants have, which are used to carry sugar-rich sap up and down the tree.

Photosynthesis

The process that trees and other plants use to harness the Sun's energy in order to turn carbon dioxide into glucose – a vital plant food.

Pneumatophore

A special root in mangrove trees that absorbs oxygen from the air.

Pollen

A dustlike substance containing male cells that is produced by plants, including trees. Pollen is used to fertilize female cells so that seeds can then be formed.

Pollination

The transfer of pollen from the male part of a flower to the female part. Some tree flowers can pollinate themselves, but in most cases the pollen must travel from one tree to another.

R

Rainforest

A forest that has at least 8 ft (2.4 m) of rain a year, spread evenly throughout the year. Tropical rainforests grow near the equator, and temperate rainforests thrive in cooler parts of the world.

Rhizomorph

A collection of feeding threads in a fungus that looks like a root. Rhizomorphs attack and kill the cells of living wood.

S

Sapwood

The wood near the outside of a tree's trunk. Sapwood contains lots of water and sugar-rich sap, and it is often lighter in color than heartwood, nearer the center of the tree.

Spore

A microscopic package of cells that some plants and fungi use when they reproduce. Spores are much simpler than seeds and can sometimes contain just one cell.

Stomata

Microscopic holes that allow gases to flow into and out of a leaf.

T

Taproot

The main root of a tree that grows straight down into the ground.

X

Xylem

A system of microscopic pipelines that trees and other plants use to carry water up from their roots. Trees grow new xylem cells every year, and their old xylem cells turn into wood.

Coniferous forest

Index

Acknowledgments

The publisher would like to thank: The Natural History Museum, Lee Thompson for additional picture research, Maggie Tingle for design assistance, Andrew O'Brien for DTP assistance, and special thanks to Robert Graham for his excellent research.

Additional models: Peter Griffiths

Illustrations: Janet Allis, Richard Orr, Kenneth Lilly, Halli Verrinder, and John Woodcock.

Additional photography: Peter Chadwick, Philip Dowel, Neil Fletcher, Frank Greenaway, Dave King, Kim Taylor, and Matthew Ward.

Picture credits:
Key: a=above; b=below; c=center; l=left; r=right; t=top.

Heather Angel/Biofotos: 17t, 24cl; **Ardea London:** Bob Gibbons 30cb; Nick Gordon 24br, 37tr; P. J. Green 24bl; Peter Steyn 24cr; Wardene

Weisser 23tr; **Bruce Coleman Collection:** Fred Bruemmer 16cl; Gerald Cubitt 16bl; William S. Paton 34bl; Michael Price 35tr; Kim Taylor 39tr; Konrad Wothe 33br; Gunter Ziesler 18tr; **ICCE Photolibrary:** S. Yorath 10bl; **Oxford Scientific Films:** Niall Benvie 22cr; J. A. L. Cooke 27tr, 36cl; Stan Osolinski 28cl; David Thompson 34cl; **Planet Earth Pictures:** D. Barrett 23tl; Richard Coomber 10cl; Hans Christian Heap 40cl; W. B. Irwin 31tr; Richard

Matthews 28cr; **Science Photo Library:** Dr. Jeremy Burgess 18cl; **Woodfall Wild Images:** 18bl.

Jacket: Tony Stone/Getty Images: Michael Busselle front b.

Index: Chris Bernstein